A NavPress Bible study on the book of

TITUS

A MINISTRY OF THE NAVIGATORS
P.O. Box 6000, Colorado Springs, CO 80934

The Navigators is an international Christian organization. Jesus Christ gave His followers the Great Commission to go and make disciples (Matthew 28:19). The aim of The Navigators is to help fulfill that commission by multiplying laborers for Christ in every nation.

NavPress is the publishing ministry of The Navigators. NavPress publications are tools to help Christians grow. Although publications alone cannot make disciples or change lives, they can help believers learn biblical discipleship, and apply what they learn to their lives and ministries.

ISBN 08910-90630

Printed in the United States of America

3 4 5 6 7 8 9 10 11 12 13 14 15 / 00 99 98 97 96 95

CONTENTS

ACKNOWLEDGMENTS

This LIFECHANGE study has been produced through the coordinated efforts of a team of Navigator Bible study developers and NavPress editorial staff, along with a nationwide network of fieldtesters.

SERIES EDITOR: KAREN HINCKLEY

HOW TO USE THIS STUDY

Objectives

Each guide in the LIFECHANGE series of Bible studies covers one book of the Bible. Although the LIFECHANGE guides vary with the individual books they explore, they share some common goals:

1. To provide you with a firm foundation of understanding and a thirst to return to the book;
2. To teach you by example how to study a book of the Bible without structured guides;
3. To give you all the historical background, word definitions, and explanatory notes you need, so that your only other reference is the Bible;
4. To help you grasp the message of the book as a whole;
5. To teach you how to let God's Word transform you into Christ's image.

Each lesson in this study is designed to take 60 to 90 minutes to complete on your own. The guide is based on the assumption that you are completing one lesson per week, but if time is limited you can do half a lesson per week or whatever amount allows you to be thorough.

Flexibility

LIFECHANGE guides are flexible, allowing you to adjust the quantity and depth of your study to meet your individual needs. The guide offers many optional questions in addition to the regular numbered questions. The optional questions, which appear in the margins of the study pages, include the following:

Optional Application. Nearly all application questions are optional; we hope you will do as many as you can without overcommitting yourself.

For Thought and Discussion. Beginning Bible students should be able to handle these, but even advanced students need to think about them. These questions frequently deal with ethical issues and other biblical principles. They often offer cross-references to spark thought, but the references do not give obvious answers. They are good for group discussions.

For Further Study. These include: a) cross-references that shed light on a topic the book discusses, and b) questions that delve deeper into the passage. You can omit them to shorten a lesson without missing a major point of the passage.

(Note: At the end of lessons four through seven you are given the option of outlining the passage just studied. Although the outline is optional, you will almost surely find it worthwhile.)

If you are meeting in a group, decide together which optional questions to prepare for each lesson, and how much of the lesson you will cover at the next meeting. Normally, the group leader should make this decision, but you might let each member choose his own application questions.

As you grow in your walk with God, you will find the LIFECHANGE guide growing with you—a helpful reference on a topic, a continuing challenge for application, a source of questions for many levels of growth.

Overview and Details

The guide begins with an overview of the book. The key to interpretation is context—what is the whole passage or book *about*?—and the key to context is purpose—what is the author's *aim* for the whole work? In lesson one you will lay the foundation for your study by asking yourself, Why did the author (and God) write the book? What did they want to accomplish? What is the book about?

Then, in lesson two, you will begin analyzing successive passages in detail. Thinking about how a paragraph fits into the overall goal of the book will help you to see its purpose. Its purpose will help you see its meaning. Frequently reviewing a chart or outline of the book will enable you to make these connections.

Finally, in the last lesson, you will review the whole book, returning to the big picture to see whether your view of it has changed after closer study. Review will also strengthen your grasp of major issues and give you an idea of how you have grown from your study.

Kinds of Questions

Bible study on your own—without a structured guide—follows a progression. First you observe: What does the passage *say*? Then you interpret: What does the passage *mean*? Lastly you apply: How does this truth affect my life?

Some of the "how" and "why" questions will take some creative thinking, even prayer, to answer. Some are opinion questions without clearcut right answers; these will lend themselves to discussions and side studies.

Don't let your study become an exercise of knowledge alone. Treat the passage as God's Word, and stay in dialogue with Him as you study. Pray, "Lord, what do you want me to see here?" "Father, why is this true?" "Lord, how does this apply to my life?"

It is important that you write down your answers. The act of writing clarifies your thinking and helps you to remember.

Meditating on verses is an option in several lessons. Its purpose is to let biblical truth sink into your inner convictions so that you will increasingly be able to act on this truth as a natural way of life. You may want to find a quiet place to spend five minutes each day repeating the verse(s) to yourself. Think about what each word, phrase, and sentence means to you. During the rest of the day, remind yourself of the verse(s) at intervals.

Study Aids

A list of reference materials, including a few notes of explanation to help you make good use of them, begins on page 80. This guide is designed to include enough background to let you interpret with just your Bible and the guide. Still, if you want more information on a subject or want to study a book on your own, try the references listed.

Scripture Versions

Unless otherwise indicated, the Bible quotations in this guide are from the New International Version of the Bible. Other versions cited are the Revised Standard Version (RSV), the King James Version (KJV), and the New American Standard Bible (NASB).

Use any translation you like for study, preferably more than one. A paraphrase such as The Living Bible is not accurate enough for study, but it can be helpful for comparison or devotional reading.

Memorizing and Meditating

A Psalmist wrote, "I have hidden your word in my heart that I might not sin against you" (Psalm 119:11). If you write down a verse or passage that challenges or encourages you, and reflect on it often for a week or more, you will find it beginning to affect your motives and actions. We forget quickly what we read once; we remember what we ponder.

When you find a significant verse or passage, you might copy it onto a card to keep with you. Set aside five minutes during each day just to think about what the passage might mean in your life. Recite it over to yourself, exploring its meaning. Then, return to your passage as often as you can during your day, for a brief review. You will soon find it coming to mind spontaneously.

For Group Study

A group of four to ten people allows the richest discussions, but you can adapt this guide for other sized groups. It will suit a wide range of group types, such as home Bible studies, growth groups, youth groups, and businessmen's studies.

Both new and experienced Bible students, new and mature Christians, will benefit from the guide. You can omit or leave for later years any questions you find too easy or too hard.

The guide is intended to lead a group through one lesson per week. However, feel free to split lessons if you want to discuss them more thoroughly. Or, omit some questions in a lesson if preparation or discussion time is limited. You can always return to this guide for personal study later on. You will be able to discuss only a few questions at length, so choose some for discussion and others for background. Make time at each discussion for members to ask about anything that gave them trouble.

Each lesson in the guide ends with a section called *For the Group*. These sections give advice on how to focus a discussion, how you might apply the lesson in your group, how you might shorten a lesson, and so on. The group leader should read each *For the Group* at least a week ahead so that he or she can tell the group how to prepare for the next lesson.

Each member should prepare for a meeting by writing answers for all the background and discussion questions to be covered. If the group decides not to take an hour per week for private preparation, then expect to take at least two meetings per lesson to work through the questions. Application will be very difficult, however, without private thought and prayer.

Two reasons for studying in a group are accountability and support. When each member commits in front of the rest to seek growth in an area of life, you can pray with one another, listen jointly for God's guidance, help one another to resist temptation, assure each other that the other's growth matters to you, use the group to practice spiritual principles, and so on. Pray about one another's commitments and needs at most meetings. Spend the first few minutes of each meeting sharing any results from applications prompted by previous lessons. Then discuss new applications toward the end of the meeting. Follow such sharing with prayer for these and other needs.

If you write down each other's applications and prayer requests, you are more likely to remember to pray for them during the week, ask about them next meeting, and notice answered prayers. You might want to get a notebook for prayer requests and discussion notes.

Notes taken during discussion will help you to remember, follow up on ideas, stay on the subject, and clarify a total view of an issue. But don't let note-taking keep you from participating. Some groups choose one member at each meeting to take notes. Then someone copies the notes and distributes them at the next meeting. Rotating these tasks can help include people. Some groups have someone take notes on a large pad of paper or erasable marker board (preformed shower wallboard works well), so that everyone can see what has been recorded.

Page 83 lists some good sources of counsel for leading group studies. The *Small Group Letter,* published by NavPress, is unique, offering insights from experienced leaders each month.

BACKGROUND

Paul and Titus

Map of the Roman Empire

Paul wrote this letter to Titus at the end of nearly thirty years as a missionary of Christ. He was born in the first decade AD in Tarsus, a small but prosperous city on the trade route from Syria to Asia Minor. His family must have owned property and had some importance in the community, for Paul was born not only a citizen of Tarsus (Acts 21:39) but even a citizen of Rome (Acts 22:27-28).[1]

Tarsus was known for its schools of philosophy and liberal arts, and some scholars believe Paul must have had some contact with these. Like most cities in the Empire, Tarsus probably contained synagogues of Greek-speaking Jews who were often as devout as their Hebrew-speaking brethren.[2] However, based on Philippians 3:5, F. F. Bruce believes that Paul's parents

Timeline of Paul's Ministry

(All dates are approximate, based on F.F. Bruce, *Paul: Apostle of the Heart Set Free*, page 475.)

Public ministry of Jesus	28-30 AD
Conversion of Paul (Acts 9:1-19)	33
Paul visits Jerusalem to see Peter (Galatians 1:18)	35
Paul in Cilicia and Syria (Galatians 1:21, Acts 9:30)	35-46
Paul visits Jerusalem to clarify the mission to the Gentiles (Galatians 2:1-10)	46
Paul and Barnabas in Cyprus and Galatia (Acts 13-14)	47-48
Letter to the Galatians	48?
Council of Jerusalem (Acts 15)	49
Paul and Silas travel from Antioch to Asia Minor, Macedonia, and Achaia (Acts 16-17)	49-50
Letters to the Thessalonians	50
Paul in Corinth (Acts 18:1-18)	50-52
Paul visits Jerusalem	52
Paul in Ephesus (Acts 19)	52-55
Letters to the Corinthians	55-56
Paul travels to Macedonia, Dalmatia, and Achaia (Acts 20)	55-57
Letter to the Romans	early 57
Paul to Jerusalem (Acts 21:1-23:22)	May 57
Paul imprisoned in Caesarea (Acts 23:23-26:32)	57-59
Paul sent to house arrest in Rome (Acts 27:1-28:31)	59-62
Letters to Philippians, Colossians, Ephesians, Philemon	60?-62
Letters to Timothy and Titus	?
Paul executed in Rome	65?

spoke Hebrew and raised him in a strict Jewish home, isolated as much as possible from the pagan city around them.[3]

Paul the Pharisee

Paul was sent to study Jewish law in Jerusalem under the foremost rabbi of his day, the Pharisee Gamaliel (Acts 22:3, Galatians 1:14). The word *Pharisee* comes from a Hebrew word meaning "the separated ones," for the Pharisees felt God had set them apart to live by the *Torah* (the Law, or Teaching, of Moses) and the oral interpretations of the Torah laid down by generations of teachers. Some Pharisees held that a man was righteous if he had done more good than bad, but Paul apparently followed the stricter group who insisted that every least implication of the Law must be kept.[4]

The Pharisees expected a *Messiah* (Hebrew for "Anointed One"; Greek: *Christ*), who would deliver them from foreign oppression and rule with justice. However, Jesus of Nazareth had scandalized many Pharisees by interpreting the Law with great freedom and claiming a special relationship with God. Thus, when some Jews began to proclaim Jesus as Messiah and Lord (a term usually reserved for God), strict Pharisees opposed them furiously.

Paul helped to lead the fight against the proclaimers of Christ in Jerusalem (Acts 7:60-8:3, Galatians 1:13). But after a couple of years, Jesus confronted Paul in a blinding encounter (Acts 9:1-19), revealing to Paul that he was persecuting the very God he professed to worship. Paul's life now turned from a Pharisaic observance of God's Law to a devoted obedience to Jesus Christ, the revealed Messiah. He joined the Jews who were urging other Jews to believe in Jesus, and after some years God called him to proclaim Jesus as Savior to Gentiles (non-Jews) also.

Paul the church leader

Paul's conversion may have marked his first move from cloistered Judaism into pagan culture. He spent ten years in Cilicia and Syria (Galatians 1:21), probably preaching Jesus along with Hellenistic (Greek-speaking) Jewish Christians who had fled Jerusalem. Then Barnabas called Paul from Tarsus to Antioch, where by this time the church was more Gentile than Jewish.[5]

Barnabas and Paul went to Jerusalem around 46 AD to settle any questions about what they were preaching (Galatians 2:1-10). Paul submitted to the authority of the Jerusalem apostles, and they acknowledged his authority.

Titus

Paul brought a companion on this Jerusalem trip: a young Gentile named Titus, whom Paul was training to carry on his ministry. When false teachers were later urging the Galatians to obey Jewish laws, Paul pointed out that the apostles had not even asked that Titus be circumcised (Galatians 2:3-5).

Paul the missionary

Soon after the Jerusalem trip, the church at Antioch commissioned Paul and Barnabas to evangelize Cyprus and Galatia. Then they attended a council at Jerusalem to settle the status of Gentiles in Christianity. Paul and Barnabas separated soon after, and Paul traveled from Antioch through Asia Minor to Macedonia and Achaia. Titus may have accompanied him on these journeys.

After this, Paul spent three years in Ephesus, and then began to travel again. In cities like Corinth and Ephesus, Paul's strategy for evangelism had been to arrive with a team of co-workers (such as Barnabas, Silas, Timothy, and Titus). With them and any Christians in the city, Paul set up a headquarters for evangelism. He and his team made converts and trained local leaders. Eventually the team left town, entrusting a network of house-churches to the local leaders.

Paul's team established the Corinthian church about 50-52 AD, but in 55 AD Paul received news of upheaval there. He wrote (1 Corinthians); he sent Timothy; he went himself; he was rejected. At last he sent Titus with a "stinging letter" (see 2 Corinthians 2:3-4).[6] This letter, which has not survived, evidently produced a change of heart, for Titus brought news of repentance (2 Corinthians 2:12-13, 7:5-7). Soon Titus bore a loving response from Paul to Corinth—the letter we call 2 Corinthians (2 Corinthians 8:17). It seems that by this time Titus was an emissary suitable for delicate matters.

Paul and Titus presumably worked together for some while longer. Paul made another missionary journey, but a trip to Jerusalem landed him in prison first in Caesarea and then in Rome (57-62 AD). Where was Titus? We do not know. Paul was released from house arrest in Rome in 62 AD, probably either to freedom or exile.[7] His letter to Titus suggests that he was in Crete at some point. When Paul wrote 2 Timothy, either shortly before or after writing to Titus, Titus was in Dalmatia (2 Timothy 4:10). Soon after writing these letters, Paul was rearrested, returned to Rome, tried, and executed.

Crete

We know nothing about the church in Crete other than what the letter to Titus tells us. In fact, any information about life in Crete at this time is scarce. But we presume that the Cretan church was founded among urban Gentiles, raised in the pagan culture of the Empire.

1. F.F. Bruce, *Paul: Apostle of the Heart Set Free* (Grand Rapids, Michigan: William B. Eerdmans Publishing Company, 1977), pages 32-40.
2. A. T. Robertson, "Paul, the Apostle," *The International Standard Bible Encyclopaedia,* volume IV (Grand Rapids, Michigan: William B. Eerdmans Publishing Company, 1956), page 2276.
3. Bruce, pages 41-43.
4. Bruce, pages 50-52.
5. Bruce, pages 127-133.
6. Bruce, page 274.
7. Bruce, pages 444-446.

LESSON ONE

OVERVIEW

Left behind in Crete, Titus had a difficult task. Anyone who has been involved in reform or change knows what Titus was facing. Think what *your* response might be to a letter from a trusted friend or a pastor while in the midst of such a task.

First impressions

Read the book of Titus through at one sitting, as a letter from a friend, before going any further. Potentially confusing verses will be clearer later if you can see how they fit into Paul's overall message. You might want to read the letter again, perhaps comparing different translations.

1. Describe the *mood* (tone, feeling) of the letter. (Is Paul formal, intimate, angry, joyful . . .?) If you think the mood changes anywhere, note where it changes.

____

____

____

____

____

____

2. What do you notice about the *style* of this letter? (Is Paul describing, giving instructions, trying to persuade . . .? Is he writing a story, a personal message, a sermon . . .?)

____

____

____

____

____

3. *Repetition* is a clue to the ideas a writer considers most important to his message. What words or ideas occur over and over in this letter?

____

____

____

____

____

____

Broad outline

4. Reread the letter, preferably in a different translation. This time, think of a short phrase or sentence to describe what you think each main section is about. (Below are the divisions according to the NIV. Feel free to change them or add more.)

1:1-4 ____

____

____

1:5-16 _______________________________________

____

____

2:1-15 ________________________________

____

____

3:1-11 ________________________________

____

____

3:12-15 ________________________________

____

____

Background

5. Read the background on Paul and Titus on pages 9-12 if you have not already done so.

> **Study Skill—Cross-references**
> Other passages of Scripture can often shed light on what you are studying. These are called *cross-references.*

6. Read 2 Corinthians 2:13, 8:23, and Titus 1:4. Summarize what these verses tell you about Paul's relationship to Titus.

____

____

____

____

____

____

____

7. What do you learn about Titus' character from the following passages in 2 Corinthians?

7:13-15 ______________________________

____

____

8:16-17 ______________________________

____

____

12:17-18 ______________________________

____

____

Purpose/themes

8. From Titus 1:5-2:1, briefly describe the situation that evidently prompted Paul to write to Titus.

____

____

____

____

____

____

____

9. What do you think are the main *themes* of this letter? (What was Paul trying to get across to Titus?) Your answer to questions 3 and 4 may point to some themes.

____

____

____

____

10. Looking for an author's *purpose* in his writing can usually help us find his main message. How would you summarize your current impression of Paul's purpose in this letter?

Your response

11. In your initial reading of Paul's letter to Titus, you may have come across concepts you'd like clarified, or you may have thought of questions you'd like answered as you go more deeply into this study. While your thoughts are still fresh, you may want to jot down your questions here to serve as personal objectives for your study of the letter.

Optional Application: One way to let a truth sink in is to tell someone else about it. To whom could you explain the most significant thing you noticed in your reading of Titus?

Study Skill—Application

The last step of Bible study is asking yourself, "What difference should this passage make in my life? How should it make me want to think or act?" Application will require time, thought, prayer, and perhaps even discussion with another person.

There are a variety of ways to approach application. At one time you might list as many implications of a scripture as you can. You can look back at this list frequently for several days and think about ways to act on the implications. At another time, you might concentrate on one specific application, giving it careful thought and prayer and committing yourself to it. At another time you might just meditate on something the scripture says about God, giving Him thanks and worship and asking Him to teach you to know Him better.

12. Did anything in your first reading of Titus especially encourage you to change or persevere in some area of your life? If so, write down this insight here, along with any implications you think it should have for your life. In prayer, consider whether there is anything you can do to act on these implications with God's help.

____

____

____

____

____

____

For the group

The beginning of a new study is a good time to lay a foundation for honest sharing of ideas, for getting comfortable with each other, and for encouraging a sense of common purpose. One way to establish common ground is to talk about what each group member hopes to get out of your group—out of your study of Titus, and out of any prayer, singing, sharing, service, outreach, or anything else you might do together. You could take about fifteen minutes at the beginning of your meeting to give each person a chance to express his or her vision for the group. If you have someone write down each member's hopes and expectations, then you can look back at these goals later to see if they are being met.

After that, you might approach your overview in the following way:

First impressions of the book (questions 1-3)—10 minutes
Background on Paul and Titus (questions 5-7)—5 minutes
Outline (question 4)—5 minutes
Themes and goals (questions 8-10)—10 minutes
Group members' questions (question 11)—5 minutes
Examples of how you might apply something in Titus (for members who are less familiar with doing this)—10 minutes

Don't feel you must follow this structure or its time allotments rigidly; it is just a model for how to go about structuring a discussion. Also, be aware that some people are better than others at outlining, seeing themes, and so on. Some people are better at close analysis of a verse, or at seeing how a scripture applies to their lives. Give thanks for each other's strengths, and don't be embarrassed to give and request help.

Traveling Teachers

Travel was safe in the Roman Empire, and knowledge of the exotic, the mysterious, and the sophisticated was prized everywhere. Accordingly, a steady stream of wandering teachers and prophets circulated among the cities. They promised skills for success, the secret of the good life,

(continued on page 20)

(continued from page 19)

higher wisdom, or worship of the true god. Some arrived with shaven heads and colored robes, bearing an idol on a litter. Others came in the simple robe, full beard, and sandals of the traditional philosopher. Some prophesied ecstatically in the streets or shouted at passers-by. Some worked miracles and healings. Others gave stirring speeches, and still others taught quietly, but all worked in public places where they could find followers.

People loved to hear new things, but only because they wanted to be entertained or to escape their daily lives. They were used to experimenting with a new philosophy or cult whenever an old one lost its freshness or seemed not to be producing the desired results.[1]

1. Ramsay MacMullen, *Paganism in the Roman Empire* (New Haven: Yale University Press, 1981), pages 1-48. For a fascinating first-hand view of the religious and social world of the Roman Empire, see *The Golden Ass* by Lucius Apuleius, translated by Robert Graves (New York: Farrar, Strauss, and Giroux, 1951); this is a wonderful novel, written in the second century AD, and the Graves edition is an inexpensive paperback.

LESSON TWO

TITUS 1:1-4

The Sent One

Have you ever been sent on a mission? Paul received his commission in a miraculous experience from the Lord Himself. Titus' commission was perhaps less dramatic, but still important. Paul wanted to remind Titus of their common mission, to encourage him in his task.

Before you begin to study 1:1-4, look back at the title you gave it in lesson one and your statements of the letter's themes and purpose. Then, carefully read 1:1-4 several times, in several different translations if possible.

This study guide defines some of the words in the passage; find in a dictionary any other words you are unsure of, and write their meanings in the margin here.

Study Skill—Diagraming

Paul often writes in long, complex sentences. One way to find the meaning of a complex sentence is to divide the sentence into phrases and draw a picture showing how the phrases relate to each other. Then you can study each phrase in turn and follow the logic between phrases.

On the next page, you will find a diagram of Titus 1:1. (You might draw it differently.) Notice how the diagram traces Paul's train of thought by showing the relationships between the phrases.

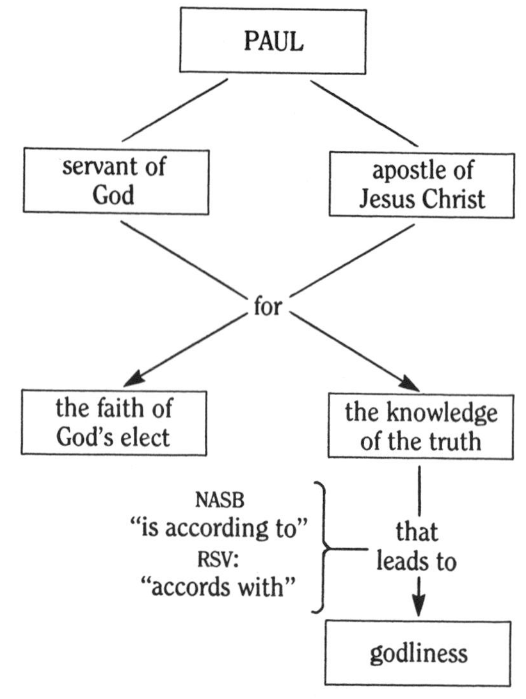

Diagram of Titus 1:1

The picture shows that *Paul* is the focus of the verse; he is describing who he believes he is. Next it shows his two titles: *servant* and *apostle*. Third comes the connecting word *for*, which tells how the next two phrases relate to Paul's titles.

Servant (verse 1). Literally, a slave owned by his master.

Apostle (verse 1). Literally, "one who is sent"—a messenger, proxy, ambassador. In Jewish law, this was the *shaliach*, "a person acting with full authority for another."[1]

The early Church recognized certain men who had seen the risen Jesus as apostles—the leaders with the highest authority regarding doctrine and policy. (See Acts 1:1-8,21-26; 6:1-6; Galatians 2:7-10.)

1. What do you think Paul wants to communicate to Titus by the way he describes himself in Titus 1:1?

____

____

____

____

____

____

Faith (verse 1). "The main elements in faith . . . are (1) a firm conviction, producing a full acknowledgment of God's revelation or truth . . . ; (2) a personal surrender to Him . . . ; (3) a conduct inspired by such surrender."[2] (See, for instance, Romans 3:21-26; 2 Corinthians 5:7; Galatians 2:20; Colossians 1:21-23; Hebrews 11:1,6; James 2:14-26.)

Godliness (verse 1). ". . . a personal attitude toward God that results in actions that are pleasing to God." "Devotion in action."[3]

2. a. NIV speaks of "the truth that leads to godliness." NASB translates, "which is according to godliness," and RSV reads, "which accords with godliness." What do you think this truth is? (See, for example, Romans 1:18-25; or John 14:6-7,15-17; or John 17:1,6-8,17.)

____

____

____

____

____

____

For Further Study: Using a concordance (see page 81), do a word study on *faith.* You might investigate how Jesus spoke of it in the Gospels, or what Paul meant by "justification by faith," or some other aspect. You could begin with the passages noted in the definition of faith on this page.

For Thought and Discussion: Read Galatians 2:20 and Hebrews 11:1-6. What is your *faith*? What does the word mean to you, and how does it affect your outlook on life?

b. In what sense does this truth accord with or lead to godliness?

3. Does Titus 1:2-3 show you any aspects of the faith and truth that motivated Paul? If so, what seems important to you in those verses?

4. Notice whom Paul calls "Savior" in verses 3 and 4. What do you learn about the nature of God from these two verses?

Grace (verse 4). God's unmerited favor to humanity. It can mean the gift of blotting out our sins through Christ, but here Paul probably means "the enabling grace for daily Christian living which is given to the saint yielded to and dependent upon the Holy Spirit."[4]

Peace (verse 4). Peace is a trait of the Messianic Age foretold by the prophets. It means wholeness and well-being in all creation—man and nature flourishing and perfect. This is wholeness in all aspects of life—physical, psychological, social, political, and so on. Thus, to wish someone "peace" is to wish him God's presence, and the personal fulfillment, completeness, and wholeness that flow only from that presence.[5]

For Thought and Discussion: **Paul often introduced a letter with comments relevant to the letter's message. Do you think Titus 1:1-4 relates to this letter's themes in any way? If so, how?**

Study Skill—Paraphrasing

Paraphrasing—putting a passage of Scripture into your own words—helps you to be sure that you understand it.

5. Now that you have examined the pieces of Paul's greeting, try to restate it in your own words.

____

____

____

____

____

____

____

____

____

6. Paul says in Titus 1:1 that knowing the truth leads to godliness. If we sometimes find our-

Optional Application: Read the paragraph on meditating on page 7. Then, memorize all or part of 1:1-4, and meditate on it for the next week. Thank God for His character and acts. As they occur to you, keep a list of implications the verses have for your life.

selves unable to act in a godly manner, then what guidance does 1:1 offer as to why we are unable to do so?

7. a. Did you discover anything in this lesson that you would like to let take hold of your thoughts and actions? If so, you might write down what seems most important to you.

b. Take a few minutes to consider what this discovery implies for your life. (How might it affect you if you let it?) Ask God to show you.

8. List any questions you have about this lesson—about what the passage means, how to apply it to yourself, and so forth.

____

____

____

____

____

Optional Application: Plan to tell some particular person the most significant thing you learned from this lesson. Plan to explain what is significant, and how it applies to you.

For the group

As a warmup for discussing this lesson, you might ask each group member to describe a time in his or her life when someone sent him or her to convey a message on that person's behalf. The event may have been as minor as a child relaying a message between parents or as important as a proxy testifying in court. This exercise should bring out some of the significance of the word *apostle*.

Don't feel you must go over each question exactly as worded in this study guide. Instead, you might start your discussion of Titus 1:1-4 by asking someone to summarize it (question 5). Then you could restate the rest of the lesson something like this:

What did you learn about what being an apostle meant to Paul?

What is "the truth that leads to godliness"? What does Titus 1:1-4 say about it? What do you know about it from elsewhere in Scripture? How does it motivate you to be godly? What does godliness mean to you?

What can we learn about God from this passage?

What was the most significant thing you learned from this passage? How does it make a difference to your life?

At the end of your meeting, you might respond to your study together by thanking God for His character as Savior; His faithfulness to His promises; His gifts of grace, peace, His Son, and the apostles; and so on.

The "One God" of Paganism

The notion of one Power governing the whole cosmos fit well with the Empire's vision of one world social, political, and economic order. A single deity behind all the cults explained their common features. Concepts of that deity varied, however. Some people imagined one hierarchy of divine beings, perhaps with a supreme god at the top. Others thought of one god with many names. Stoic philosophy described the impersonal force of the *Logos,* Highest Reason, by which the cosmos functioned. Stoics taught that man must know and conform to the ethical principles of that Reason in order to live well, for *Logos,* not human choice, determined all events. Finally, some people believed in *Tyche,* the personified Fate who was not blind but irrational and malevolent.

1. Erich von Eicken and Helgo Lindner, "Apostle," *The New International Dictionary of New Testament Theology,* volume 1, edited by Colin Brown (Grand Rapids, Michigan: Zondervan Corporation, 1975), page 128.
2. W. E. Vine, *Vine's Expository Dictionary of New Testament Words* (Nashville, Tennessee: Royal Publishers, 1952), page 401.
3. Jerry Bridges, *The Practice of Godliness* (Colorado Springs, Colorado: NavPress, 1983), page 18.
4. Kenneth S. Wuest, *First Peter in the Greek New Testament* (Grand Rapids, Michigan: William B. Eerdmans Publishing Company, 1942), page 17.
5. Harmut Beck and Colin Brown, "Peace," *The New International Dictionary of New Testament Theology,* volume 2, pages 776-783; Markus Barth, *Ephesians 1-3,* Anchor Bible volume 34 (Garden City, New York: Doubleday and Company, 1974), page 74.

LESSON THREE

TITUS 1:5-9

Titus' Mission

Leaders. What is their job in the Church, and what should they be like? The Church has changed a lot in two millenia, but Paul's counsel to Titus can still guide us in choosing and training leaders.

Pray for concentration and discernment. Then read this passage several times, using several translations if possible. Keep in mind that it is God's life-giving and life-transforming Word you are investigating.

1. For what two purposes did Paul send Titus to Crete (verse 5)?

___

___

___

___

___

Elders (verse 5). See the box, "Church Leadership" on pages 36-37.

2. a. What trait did Paul repeat in verses 6 and 7 to describe a truly qualified church elder?

___

b. What do you think this word means?

Study Skill—Understanding Words

Defining a word can serve several purposes. First, just stopping to consider what it means and finding it in a dictionary can help you to think about it. You will notice its importance and remember it later. Second, a definition may throw some new light on a verse—either a familiar or an unfamiliar one.

An English dictionary will define the word used in your translation; this may be enough help. A Bible dictionary or dictionary of New Testament words will define the Greek word behind the translation. It will often give a literal definition and then some commentary about the word's significance in the New Testament.

3. According to 1:6-9, what qualities equip a person to lead in the Body of Christ? (If you don't understand some of the words in your translation, consult another version or a good English dictionary.)

4. What do you think Paul meant by "husband of one wife" (verse 6)? (For instance, do you think he was excluding bachelors from leadership? Was he excluding men who had been polygamists before conversion, as was acceptable in many parts of the Empire? Was he forbidding second marriages? Explain why you interpret as you do.) See 1 Corinthians 7:8-9,32-35.

____

____

____

____

5. Why do you think an elder's moral standard is important? (See Titus 2:7, 1 Timothy 3:4-7.)

____

____

____

____

____

6. a. In your own words, explain what Paul expected of an elder's children (Titus 1:6).

____

____

____

____

b. Why is the belief and behavior of an elder's children a qualification for leadership (1 Timothy 3:4-5)?

____

____

____

____

For Thought and Discussion:
a. Alcoholism, marital unfaithfulness, and other sins can overcome even committed, believing Christian leaders. What do you think a church can do to help its leaders resist such temptations? (See, for example, 1 Thessalonians 5:11-14.)

b. What should a church do if it discovers that one of its leaders has fallen in one of these ways? (See Matthew 18:15-17 and 1 Timothy 5:19-20. On unrepentant sinners, see 1 Corinthians 5:1-2,5-6,13. On repentant sinners, see 2 Corinthians 2:6-8 and Galatians 6:1-4.)

7. Why do you think even temper is important for a Christian leader (*Optional*: See James 1:19-20; Ephesians 4:1-3,26-27,31-32)?

Encourage (Titus 1:9). Or, "exhort" (NASB, KJV). To remind a person of previously taught knowledge in order to influence him to act upon it. Encouragement/exhortation addresses the intellect, will, and emotions. Its methods range from a gentle "you can do it" to an urgent "get moving!" The Greek verb *parakaleo* is related to the noun *paraklete*, the title given the Holy Spirit in John 14:16.

8. a. What is "the trustworthy message" (verse 9; NASB: "the faithful word"; RSV: "the sure word")?

   b. Explain in your own words why a leader must "hold firmly to the trustworthy message as it has been taught" (verse 9).

c. What practical steps might a leader take to see that he is holding fast to this message?

____

____

____

____

____

____

____

9. a. Think about your own potential for some kind of leadership. In which areas listed in verses 6-9 are you probably strongest?

____

____

____

____

____

____

b. In which are you probably weakest?

____

____

____

____

____

____

____

10. If you are a leader or teacher in your church, how does 1:5-9 help you to understand what your job and character should be? (If you are

Optional Application: Think about why you are weak in one of the areas you listed in question 9b. Pray for grace to change in this matter, and ask God to reveal any action or change in attitude that you might pursue. You may want to pray about this consistently and patiently for a while. Write down any insight you receive from your prayer.

Optional Application: Study the following cross-references, and write down anything you can do to work on one of the areas of weakness you identified in question 9b. (Psalm 1:1-2; Romans 6:6,11; 2 Corinthians 10:5; James 5:16; 1 John 1:9.)

Optional Application: Think of some leader in your church who is especially strong in one or more of the areas listed in verses 6-9. How can you let this person know that you recognize and appreciate his qualifications in this area? What could you say or write to him?

not a leader or teacher, how does it help you to understand better the responsibilities of leaders over you?)

____

____

____

____

____

____

____

Study Skill—Changing Character

Sometimes the Bible commands a character trait, an attitude, or a habit which we find we cannot adopt by an act of effort or even much prayer. You may feel this is true about some of the traits listed in Titus 1:6-9. One problem might be the "old self."

Before we knew Christ, we believed lies about how the world worked. We made choices based on those lies and built up a structure of habits and responses. Now that we know Christ, we have rejected those lies, but the structure remains. Paul talks about this predicament in Romans 7:22-24. He says that our only route to freedom from this structure is "through Jesus Christ our Lord" (Romans 7:25). We must let Him nail to the Cross the "old self" (Romans 6:6, Ephesians 4:22-24), the structure which fights to live on in our members. Letting Him do this involves asking Him to do it, giving Him permission to do it, having others pray for us (James 5:16), and acting in faith that God really has answered our prayer for freedom (Romans 8:2).[1]

11. Is there one particular truth from your study of 1:5-9 that you would like to concentrate on in your own life? If so, write it down here, along with one practical way you could begin to make it part of you with God's help.

You may find that as you study Paul's letter more closely, your view of its overall message will change. If so, feel free to make up a new statement of the purpose of this letter.

12. Recall from question 11 in lesson one (page 17) what you thought Paul's reason for writing this letter was. How does 1:5-9 fit into that purpose? (In other words, what seems to be the point of 1:5-9?)

13. List any questions you have about 1:5-9.

For the group

You could begin your meeting by asking each member to think of someone he or she has known whose life illustrates one of the traits Paul says an elder should have. Let each member name the trait and then give one brief example of how that person showed that trait.

When planning how to organize your discussion, consider the following steps:

Read the passage aloud
Summarize the passage.
Name each trait, define it for yourselves, and explain why you think it is important.
Provide time for members' questions.
Spend one third to one half your total time discussing how you can apply this passage to your own lives. How can the truth you know about God lead you to godliness?
Summarize your discussion.
Pray for members' personal needs, and ask God to enable you to do what He desires. You could also thank Him for each others' gifts to the group.

Church Leadership

The New Testament gives no clear picture of how churches were organized. From scattered references we can make only a probable sketch.

A group of believers met periodically, perhaps weekly, in the home of a member wealthy enough to have a spacious house (Romans 16:5). We call such a group a "house-church." This church (Greek: *ekklesia;* literally, "assembly") probably prayed, sang, and heard Scripture read and discussed (Colossians 3:16). They also ate together, celebrated the Lord's Supper, and baptized (1 Corinthians 1:13-17, 11:17-34). Poor members, widows, and orphans were cared for (1 Timothy 5:3-16). The doctrines of the faith were taught.

When Paul went to a city to evangelize, he seems to have set up headquarters in one house-church. Probably, when the first house-church outgrew its house, it divided in two. But the many churches in a city like Corinth seem to have remained connected in a way that those in Rome, which grew up independently of each

(continued on page 37)

(continued from page 36)

other, were not.[2]

Leadership roles seem not to have been strictly defined. On the one hand, the special authority of apostles was recognized by Christians everywhere (1 Corinthians 12:28), although there was some debate as to who was and was not an apostle (2 Corinthians 11:5,13; Galatians 1:11-12; 2:9). There were also prophets, evangelists, and teachers who might travel from city to city with messages from the Lord (Acts 11:27-30, 13:1; 1 Corinthians 12:28; Ephesians 4:11). *The Didache*, a manual for churches from about 70-110 AD, laid down rules for discerning true prophets and regulating the hospitality such travelers might expect.[3]

On the other hand, local churches were led day to day by elders (*presbuteroi*), deacons (*diakonoi*), overseers (or, "bishops"; *episkopoi*), pastors, and teachers (Romans 12:6-8, Ephesians 4:11, 1 Timothy 3:1-13). We do not know whether these titles denoted different ranks, but scholars tend to feel that leadership was loose and fell on those whom the group agreed to recognize.[4] These local leaders managed finances, pastoral care, doctrine, disputes, and so on. There seem to have been several in each house-church. A more formal leadership structure did not develop until the Church grew large in the second century AD.

1. John and Paula Sandford, *The Transformation of the Inner Man* (Plainfield, New Jersey: Bridge Publishing Company, 1982), pages 23-27.
2. F. F. Bruce, *New Testament History* (New York: Doubleday and Company, Inc., 1971), page 394.
3. *The Didache* is available in paperback in *Early Christian Writings*, edited by Maxwell Staniforth (New York: Penguin Books, 1968), pages 225-237.
4. Bruce, *New Testament History*, pages 405, 417-418; Henry Chadwick, *The Early Church* (New York: Penguin Books, 1967), pages 45-49.

LESSON FOUR

TITUS 1:10-16

False Teachers

God's sheep are vulnerable. There are dozens of teachers around, eager to lead us in one direction or another. They appeal to our weaknesses and make what we want to hear seem like God's Word. We need to learn to know whom we can trust and what to do about false shepherds.

Read 1:10-16 several times before beginning the questions in this lesson. Glance back at your overview of the book (questions 4, 9, and 10 of lesson one). Orienting yourself in these ways will help you see the point of this paragraph.

1. What seems to be Paul's main point in 1:10-16?

____

____

____

____

____

The Cretan character was proverbial in the ancient world. In Greek, "to Cretize" meant to lie, and a philosophical paradox was built around the statement, "All Cretans are liars, and I am a Cretan."

The "prophet" Paul mentioned in verse 12 was Epimenides, a Cretan philosopher of the sixth century BC. Most educated men of Paul's day had to study Epimenides.

2. Explain in your own words each of the characteristics Paul mentions as he describes a certain kind of teacher.

character qualities (verse 10) ______________

____

____

____

____

____

____

____

motive (verse 11) ______________

____

____

____

Circumcision group (verse 10). Throughout His ministry, Paul repeatedly confronted men who taught that to be a Christian a person had to follow all the Jewish law, including circumcision (Galatians 2:1-5,11-16; 6:12-16; Colossians 2:6-23).

3. What do you think it means to have "minds and consciences . . . corrupted" (verse 15)?

____

____

____

____

____

____

4. a. "To the pure, all things are pure" (verse 15) is a statement that could easily be abused. In what sense do you think Paul meant it?

b. How might a false teacher twist this statement to excuse sin? (See Romans 6:15, 1 Corinthians 6:12-13, 10:23-24.)

5. Why are the false teachers "unfit for doing anything good" (Titus 1:16)?

6. a. How did Paul want Titus to deal with false teachers (Titus 1:11,13)?

For Further Study: Compare what Paul says about the false teachers to what Jesus says about the Pharisees in Mark 7:5-15 and Luke 11:37-41. How are the false teachers and Pharisees alike? How are they different?

For Thought and Discussion: What is the church member's responsibility in dealing with false teachers? What is a leader's responsibility?

b. What was the goal of treating false teachers in this manner (verse 13)?

7. The word *for* in verse 10 tells how 1:10-15 relates to 1:5-9. What is the connection between the two paragraphs?

8. Titus 1:10-15 lists some clues for discerning false teachers. Choose three of these traits and explain how the qualities of a true leader (1:5-9) equip him to expose and counter each trait.

Study Skill—Connecting Words

Connecting words are clues to how passages relate to each other. They include *and, but, for, if . . . then, because, in order to,* and many other phrases.

9. Based on chapter 1, summarize the problems Titus faced in the Cretan church.

For Further Study: **Try outlining Titus 1:1-16, or experiment with just one paragraph.**

Study Skill—Outlining

When you entitle paragraphs, summarize the point of a passage, or relate passage to passage, you are trying to grasp Paul's meaning by *seeing the connection in his thoughts.*

One way to show yourself the connections in a passage is to outline it. You first summarize its main teaching in a phrase or sentence (an expanded title or purpose statement). Then you summarize its main sections (in Titus, paragraphs). Finally, you add the supporting ideas from individual verses. For instance, an outline of Titus might begin like this:

I. [The purpose, or overall message, of the book of Titus]
   A. [The main idea of Titus 1:1-4]
      1. [a supporting point]
      2.
      . . .
   B. [The main idea of Titus 1:5-9]
      1.
      2.
      . . .
   C. [The main idea of Titus 1:10-16]
      . . .

Optional Application: Does anything in 1:10-16 call to mind any practices that you need to stop? If so, describe what you might do about this conviction. Try to be specific about your response.

10. List any questions you have about anything you have studied so far.

____

____

____

____

____

____

Study Skill—Obedience

We need to apply Scripture in both of two ways. In lesson three we looked at how to deal with habits over which at first we have little control; in that case God must teach our hearts the truth (Titus 1:1) and tear down the structure based on lies. On the other hand, sometimes we already have been given the power to do what is right; in that case we need to stop stalling and obey (Romans 6:11-14, 8:12-14).

11. Have you had a particular insight from this lesson that you would like to focus on in the next week? You might want to write it down here, so that it doesn't slip out of your thoughts when you go on to the next lesson. Pray for God's leading in ways to make this truth really take hold in your life.

____

____

____

____

____

____

____

____

For the group

At your last meeting you probably committed yourselves to try to apply something from Titus 1:5-9. You might begin this meeting by each sharing briefly how your efforts to apply Titus have been going. The goal here is not to impress or shame anyone, but to encourage each other. No one should expect dramatic, permanent changes in character after one week. So don't get sidetracked on this discussion; just spend about ten minutes, and write down anyone's frustrations or questions to address and pray about later. Then move on. Look for more study skills on application later in this study guide.

A good standard structure for Bible study is the following:

Summary of the passage.
Observation—What does Paul say (about the false teachers, for instance) in this passage?
Interpretation—What do you think Paul means by . . . ?
Application—How does any of this apply to the way you behave, or to the Church today? This section should take at least a third of your time. It is also probably the best time to work through anyone's past difficulties with application.
Prayer.

The study group should be a nurturing group as well. How can you help (not push) each other to see God's truth, to fulfill your commitments to application, to grow into leaders?

Pagan Views of Body and Soul

Part of a Christian teacher's job was to replace the notions about life that people grew up with in the Roman world with "sound doctrine" (1:9). But uprooting common assumptions was no easy task.

Gentiles generally believed that matter was essentially evil, or at least inferior to spirit. Like-

(continued on page 46)

(continued from page 45)
wise, they held that man's body was crude, bad, mortal, and bestial, while his soul was divine, immortal, glorious, and untainted. People thought of themselves as immortal souls imprisoned in corrupt bodies—the soul was innocent; only the body was evil.

This dualism (sharp division of the world into good spirit and evil matter) led to two opposite extremes. On the one hand, many religions taught asceticism. Restricting sex, food, and so on was thought to detach a person from the body and so make him pure. "Sin" referred to breaking rules regarding use of the body. Sins of this kind put up barriers between a man and the gods. To approach a god, a person might purify himself through cleansing rites, asceticism, animal sacrifice, self-mutilation, or hymns of praise inscribed in public places.

On the other hand, some cults claimed that if a person underwent certain initiating rites and knew certain secrets, then he was "pure" in soul. Nothing he did with his body could then affect his soul's purity. These beliefs encouraged immorality and self-indulgence.

Almost everyone in the Empire believed that souls were immortal, although expectations about future life varied. But pagans found it hard to believe that disgusting, corrupt bodies would be resurrected (1 Corinthians 15:12-58); they could not understand what Paul meant.

LESSON FIVE

TITUS 2:1-10

Practicing Godliness

At first glance, 2:1-10 may seem like a list of rules, comforting or confining depending on your preferences. But is that all there is to this passage?

Read 2:1-10 prayerfully before beginning the questions in this lesson.

For Thought and Discussion: Paul uses an emphatic *you* in verse 1 to contrast Titus with the teachers of 1:10-16. (NASB reads, "But as for you . . . .") Based on what you learned from chapter 1, why do you think Paul counseled Titus as he did in 2:1? (Look at the overseer's job in 1:9.)

Study Skill—What's the Point?

Before you look at the details of a passage, it's usually a good idea to decide what the passage as a whole is about. To determine the point of a passage, you can ask yourself two questions: 1) what is Paul talking about in this passage, and 2) why is he saying it here (what does it have to do with what comes before and after)?[1]

1. Think about the purpose of this letter to Titus. What seems to be the point of 2:1-10, in the context of the rest of the letter?

____

____

____

____

____

2. List the qualities each of these groups of people should have. Be sure you are able to explain

what each quality means. To understand the terms, you may want to refer to other Bible versions and/or a good English dictionary.

Older men (verse 2) ______________________

____

____

____

____

____

____

____

Older women (verse 3) ____________________

____

____

____

____

____

Younger women (verses 4-5) _______________

____

____

____

____

____

____

Younger men (verse 6) ___________________

____

____

____

Slaves (verses 9-10) ______

______

______

______

3. How do you think "sound" faith, love, and endurance (verse 2) are related to "sound" doctrine (verse 1)?

______

______

______

______

4. The Greek word for "reverent" (verse 3) means the state of mind of a holy person.[2] What does this word imply to you?

______

______

______

______

______

Self-controlled (1:8; 2:2,5,6). "Sensible" in NASB. Implies clear-headedness, not being influenced by alcohol or any obsession that hinders your ability to choose freely.[3]

5. a. The word *then* in 2:4 (*that* in NASB and KJV) shows the connection between verses 3 and 4. How does verse 4 depend upon verse 3?

______

______

For Further Study:
To learn more about self-control, study the following cross-references.

a. Why is self-control important (1 Peter 4:7, 5:8)?

b. Self-control is a "fruit of the Spirit" (Galatians 5:22-23). Explain how a person obtains self-control (Galatians 5:13-24; Romans 8:5-9,12-13).

Optional Application: Assess your own level of self-control. Do any desires (for possessions, influence, approval, etc.) weaken your self-control, keep you from listening to God's will? If so, write down what they are. Is there anything you or God might do to strengthen your self-control?

____

____

____

b. Paul told Titus to do good for a similar reason in verse 7. Why is a leader's or teacher's *example* so important?

____

____

____

____

____

Study Skill—Crossing Cultures

We agree that the New Testament is God's Word to us, authoritative for our behavior. And we agree that some commands, such as Titus 3:12, were written just for their original readers. But how do we distinguish between commands we should apply as given, instructions from which we can draw principles, and instructions that were meant just for the past?

Gordon Fee offers this guideline, among others: "Whenever we share comparable particulars (i.e., similar specific life situations) with the first-century setting, God's Word to us is the same as God's Word to them."[4]

For instance, as sinners in need of redemption, we are all in the same boat. But we should be alert to recognize when our situations are different, and when the New Testament distinguishes between principle and specific application. For example, we may not need to take wine for stomach ailments (1 Timothy 5:23) or to greet each other with "a holy kiss" (Romans 16:16).

6. Do you think verses 9-10 can be applied to modern employees who work for wages? If you think they can, give one example of how. If not, why not?

7. Paul often gave reasons for the qualities he said we should have. In our English translations of this letter, these reasons are signaled by phrases such as *that, so that,* and *in order that.* At the end of verses 5, 8, and 10 are three examples of such reasons. List these three reasons below, and be able to explain why each is important.

verse 5

verse 8

verse 10

Optional Application: Does any one of the motives you named in questions 5 and 7 especially motivate you? If so, why do you find it motivating? What does it motivate you to do?

Study Skill—Motives

Sometimes a list of expectations like the one in 2:1-10 can be intimidating and demotivating. We see how far we fall short, and it seems hopeless even to try to measure up. At those times, it can help if we focus on the *reasons* Paul gives to encourage us.

8. a. Review the category of question 2 that applies to you. How might Paul's instructions be applied to your life? (You might want to focus on just one instruction.)

b. What could you do this week to seek growth in this area of your character?

9. What currently seems most important to you of all that you learned from this passage?

____

____

____

____

____

____

10. List here any questions you have about anything in 2:1-10.

____

____

____

____

Optional Application: How can you demonstrate "integrity, seriousness and soundness of speech" (verses 7-8; NASB: "purity in doctrine, dignified, sound in speech") in the ways you influence others' lives? Think about your fellow study group members, children, co-workers, and so on.

For the group

As a warmup, consider having each member briefly describe a teacher he or she had as a child whom he or she really liked and learned important things from. Why was that teacher effective?

Doing careful observation and interpretation before application is especially important in a passage like Titus 2:1-10, which gives instructions about lifestyle alongside instructions about character. Some issues that this passage often raises are:

a. Paul taught that young women should "love" and "be subject to" their husbands and should work at home, but he said nothing comparable to older women or men. Why? What does it mean to subject oneself? How does this teaching apply today? We need to see such teachings in the context of *all* that God says about roles. See, for instance, Genesis 2:18,23-24; Ephesians 5:21-33; 1 Peter 2:13, 3:1-9.

b. "Self-control" may sound like some teeth-gritting act of suppressing impulses, sanctification by one's own efforts alone. How are sinful thoughts

For Thought and Discussion: Go back to question 1, and see if you have refined your opinion of what 2:1-10 is about.

For Further Study: Even if you didn't outline chapter 1, you might try outlining 2:1-10, just to see whether it helps you organize your thoughts.

and habits uprooted? What part does God's Spirit play, and how do we cooperate? Look for Scripture references in Study Skills in this guide.

You may decide to postpone discussing issues like these for a separate meeting, after anyone interested has had time to study relevant scriptures. Or, you may discuss them now if everyone agrees.

A possible order for your discussion is:

List the character traits Paul urges for each group, and explain what they mean.
Discuss the motives Paul gives for this behavior.
Define how Paul wants Titus to teach these traits and motives.
Decide how all this applies to you. This is a good chance to discuss ethics in the workplace and in social gatherings. Be prepared for disagreement as to how Paul's teaching applies today.

Syncretism

Teachers who traveled from city to city in the Empire often claimed to know the full truth of life, but they rarely asked for conversion as we understand it. People were cosmopolitan: dozens of religions were practiced side by side in a city, and it was fine to join several cults, study with several philosophers, worship an ancestral god, and perform civic rites. Few religions demanded exclusive loyalty or claimed exclusive truth. People composed their own system of beliefs by choosing what they liked from many sources. They tended to view gods with vaguely similar traits as the same god with various names. (For instance, they equated the Asian Cybele, the Roman Diana, and the Greek Artemis, even though those goddesses were originally very different.) They borrowed a custom from one cult to worship another god. They mixed philosophies and combined them with religions. This mixing of religious ideas and practices is called *syncretism*.

In such an atmosphere, Jews and Christians seemed strange. They wanted converts to

(continued on page 55)

(continued from page 54)

renounce other philosophies and cults. Admirers who thought Zeus was the same as God the Father, or who sought Christian rites and biblical teachings alongside pagan lifestyles, found Christian stubbornness astounding.

1. Gordon D. Fee and Douglas Stuart, *How To Read the Bible for All Its Worth* (Grand Rapids, Michigan: Zondervan Corporation, 1982), page 24.
2. Donald Guthrie, *The Pastoral Epistles* (Grand Rapids, Michigan: William B. Eerdmans Publishing Company, 1982), page 192.
3. Kelly, page 66. Vine defines this word as "of sound mind" in Vine, page 1057.
4. Fee and Stuart, page 60.

LESSON SIX

TITUS 2:11-15

Sound Doctrine

We need to know *what* to do, but most of us will never get off the ground until we know *why* and *how*. Here is the gospel in a nutshell.

1. a. Carefully read through this passage several times, and reread 2:1-10. What word in 2:11-15 links this passage with the previous one?

   ____

   b. What is the connection between the two passages?

   ____

   ____

   ____

   ____

   ____

2. Paraphrase (restate in your own words) verse 11. (For instance, what is "the grace of God that brings salvation"?)

   ____

   ____

   ____

   ____

For Further Study: On Titus 2:11, see Romans 3:21-26, 2 Timothy 1:10, or Titus 3:4-7.

Optional Application: a. Think about your own struggle with "ungodliness and worldly passions." What truths in Titus 2:11-14 could help you change the attitudes behind your ungodly habits?

b. Consider meditating on verses 11-14 when you are tempted to act against what you know to be right. You could copy these verses onto a card to keep with you for quick reference.

3. How does God's grace teach us (or, "discipline" us; NASB marginal note) to deny ungodliness and worldly passions in our lives (Titus 2:11-14)? (*Optional*: See Ephesians 2:4-10, 4:1-3, 5:1-2; Romans 6:1-23, 8:2-10.)

4. a. In 2:14, Paul gives two reasons why Christ became human and let Himself be crucified—to *redeem* us and to *purify* us. Explain what you think each of these reasons means.

"redeem us from all wickedness" ____________

"purify for himself a people . . . eager to do what is good"

b. Have you experienced Christ redeeming and purifying you? If so, what have you learned about how He does this in a person's life?

5. a. What is "the blessed hope" from which all our aims and priorities should flow (2:13, 1:2)?

____

____

____

____

b. The knowledge of this truth in 2:13 should lead us to the godliness described in 2:12 and 2:14. Why do you think the truth in 2:13 should lead us to godliness?

____

____

____

____

____

6. Paul says in verse 14 that a characteristic of Christ's people is that they are "eager to do what is good." Look up the cross-references below to learn more about what Jesus says about doing good, and record your findings.

Matthew 7:21-23 ______________________________

____

____

____

____

Matthew 25:34-40 ______________________________

____

____

____

____

For Further Study: From where does a Christian leader receive his "authority" (verse 15)? See Titus 1:1-4 and 1 Corinthians 2:4-5.

For Further Study:
a. What wrong beliefs about doing good does the *older* son have in the parable of the Lost Son, Luke 15:11-32?
b. Study Jesus' words in Matthew 5:43-48 and 6:1-4.
c. Look at other passages on doing good, such as Ephesians 2:10 and James 2:14-19.
d. Study the many ways and reasons Peter gives for doing good in his first letter, especially in 1 Peter 3:8-4:19.

Luke 10:25-37 ______________________

Luke 10:38-42 ______________________

7. Are you eager to do good in the way Jesus urged? If so, how could you do so better in the next week? If you have to admit you're not eager, then how might you grow more eager?

8. What seems to be the overall point of 2:11-15, in the context of the whole letter?

Study Skill—Five Questions

The following five questions may aid you in applying God's Word. When you study a passage, try asking yourself:

Is there a *sin* for me to avoid?
Is there a *promise* for me to trust?
Is there an *example* for me to follow?
Is there a *command* for me to obey?

How can this passage increase my *knowledge* of the Lord (not just knowledge about Him)?

You can recall these five questions by remembering the acronym SPECK—Sin, Promise, Example, Command, Knowledge.

9. a. What is the most significant insight you found in 2:11-15?

____

____

____

____

____

____

b. What implications does this insight have for your life?

____

____

____

____

____

c. Is there anything practical you could do about any of these implications? Recall the Study Skills on pages 18, 34, 44, and 52.

____

____

For Further Study:
Show how 2:11-15 is organized by making up an outline or a diagram of this paragraph.

If you have been outlining all of the letter to Titus, try to show how 2:11-15 fits the overall message by the way you add this section of the outline.

10. List any questions you have about 2:11-15.

For the group

Titus 2:11-15 describes how God motivates us to be the people He wants. You could open your discussion by having everyone give one example of how their parents tried to motivate them. Then ask someone to summarize the point of 2:11-15.

"The grace of God that brings salvation" (verse 11) and "the blessed hope" (verse 13) are the bases of God's motivation. You might focus on these two ideas, first defining what they mean and then exploring how they should motivate us.

Or, after summarizing the paragraph, you could discuss: 1) What is doing good? 2) Why should we do good? 3) What in this lesson encourages or motivates group members as they seek to apply Paul's instructions? This may be a good time to discuss your successes and frustrations with application.

C. S. Lewis on Trying Hard

"Now we cannot, in that sense, discover our failure to keep God's law except by trying our very hardest (and then failing). Unless we really try, whatever we say there will always be at the back of our minds the idea that if we try harder next time we shall succeed in being completely good. Thus, in one sense, the road back to God is a road of moral effort, of trying harder and harder. But in another sense it is not trying that is ever

(continued on page 63)

(continued from page 62)
going to bring us home. All this trying leads up to the vital moment at which you turn to God and say, 'You must do this. I can't.' Do not, I implore you, start asking yourselves, 'Have I reached that moment?' Do not sit down and start watching your own mind to see if it is coming along. That puts a man quite on the wrong track. . . . What matters is the nature of the change in itself, not how we feel while it is happening. It is the change from being confident about our own efforts to the state in which we despair of doing anything for ourselves and leave it to God.

"... in a sense, you may say that no temptation is ever overcome until we stop trying to overcome it—throw up the sponge. But then you could not 'stop trying' in the right way and for the right reason until you had tried your very hardest. And, in yet another sense, handing everything over to Christ does not, of course, mean that you stop trying. To trust Him means, of course, trying to do all that He says. There would be no sense in saying you trusted a person if you would not take his advice. Thus if you have really handed yourself over to Him, it must follow that you are trying to obey Him. But trying in a new way, a less worried way. Not doing these things in order to be saved, but because He has begun to save you already. Not hoping to get to Heaven as a reward for your actions, but inevitably wanting to act in a certain way because a first faint gleam of Heaven is already inside you."[1]

1. C. S. Lewis, *Mere Christianity* (New York: Macmillan Publishing Company, 1943), pages 127-129.

LESSON SEVEN

TITUS 3:1-11

Past and Present

Paul must have known that it would be hard for Titus to teach submission to authorities in a place like Crete, where tempers were hot and political views were strong and varied. So, Paul carefully gave Titus a context in which to teach submission, and he trusted Titus to make clear what he meant.

Read 3:1-11, noticing how the passage's three paragraphs relate to one another. Think also about what this passage has to do with the rest of the letter. Pray that God will speak to you personally.

1. The word *for* in verse 3 (NASB, RSV) shows that verses 3-7 give a reason for verses 1-2. What is the connection between these two paragraphs?

____

____

____

____

____

2. What would you say 3:1-11 as a whole is about?

____

____

____

____

For Further Study: a. In a concordance, find other biblical teaching on *submission (submit, subject), authority, obey, reverence, fear,* and so on. Study what it means to be subject, and why Christians should have those attitudes. You might begin with Romans 13:1-14 and 1 Peter 2:11-17.

b. Or, do a word study on *humility (humble, gentle, meek),* or on another word in Titus 3:1-2.

Optional Application: Can you think of any ways in which you personally could apply 3:1-2 to your thoughts and actions toward authorities over you? If so, explain at least one first step you could take to begin acting on Paul's instructions.

Submission (3:1-2)

In 3:1-2, Paul says that the Cretans should be subject to authorities. In 3:3-8, he gives the doctrinal basis for being subject. It is another case of truth (doctrine) leading to godliness (attitude and behavior).

Read the box, "Submission" on pages 71-72, and think about what it meant "to be subject to rulers and authorities" (Titus 3:1) in Paul's day.

3. From Titus 3:1-2 and Acts 5:29, try to state some principles regarding what it means to be subject to authorities.

4. How might being "ready to do whatever is good" (Titus 3:1) affect a modern Christian's actions as a citizen? Try to give some specific examples.

Incentives (3:3-8)

Foolish (verse 3). Not unwise in worldly matters, but without spiritual understanding.[1] See also 1 Corinthians 1:18,21,25; 2:13-3:4.

5. How did God show His "kindness and love" to us (verses 4-5)?

6. Consider the point Paul makes in 3:4-7, especially what he says about doing good in verse 5. Why do you think he made this point after 3:1-2?

7. "Justified by his grace" (verse 7) is Paul's great slogan. Briefly, what does it mean? (See Romans 3:23-29; 5:1; 2 Corinthians 5:19,21.

For Thought and Discussion: In 3:3, Paul asserts that before knowing God "we"—including himself and Titus—were as bad as the Cretans. To what extent does verse 3 describe your past?

For Further Study:
a. What is "the washing of rebirth" (Titus 3:5; NASB: "the washing of regeneration")? See, for instance, John 1:12-13, 3:5-8, 1 Corinthians 6:11, Hebrews 10:22, 1 Peter 1:3.

b. What is the "renewal by the Holy Spirit"? See Romans 8:2,6,11,15-16; 12:2; 2 Corinthians 4:16-18; Ephesians 4:22-24; Colossians 3:10-11.

c. Or, do you think Paul means "the washing of rebirth . . . by the Holy Spirit" and "the washing of . . . renewal by the Holy Spirit"? Why do you think so?

8. We have been reborn and renewed by the Holy Spirit, says Paul (verse 5). Why should this status motivate us to "devote [our]selves to doing what is good" (verse 8)?

____

____

____

____

____

9. What does it imply for you that we are "heirs" (verse 7)? (See, for instance, Romans 8:14-17, Revelation 21:1-7.)

____

____

____

____

____

____

10. In Titus 3:8, Paul says that stressing verses 3-7 to the Cretans will prompt them to live good lives. (Remember "the truth that leads to godliness" in 1:1.) Does anything in 3:3-7 encourage you to live as in 3:1-2? If so, what do you find motivating in those verses?

____

____

____

____

____

____

____

Dealing with divisiveness (3:9-11)

11. a. What sorts of things does a "divisive person" (verse 10; NASB: "factious man") do? Study verse 9, and use a dictionary if you need to.

b. How was Titus supposed to deal with such a person (verses 9-10)?

c. From verse 11, explain why this is the best response to divisiveness.

12. a. The arguments in Crete were about "genealogies" (Jewish descent) and "the law" (how the Law of Moses applied to Christians). Few modern churches argue about these topics. Still, how might you recognize an "unprofitable and useless" (verse 9) religious discussion in your church? (*Optional:* See Romans 14:1-15:3.)

b. Describe some strategies Christians might use for avoiding unprofitable discussions and ensuring healthy ones.

13. Make a "do-list" of all the things Paul told Titus to do in 3:1-11. Or, just skim through the passage. Afterwards, choose one instruction that you think God especially wants you to take to heart this week. Consider how it applies to you, and then write out a plan for how you might begin to respond to this instruction.

14. In a sentence or two, explain how you think 3:1-11 fits into the purpose of this letter.

15. List any questions you have about 3:1-11.

For Further Study: Make up an outline of 3:1-11 that you think organizes its key points. Try to make your outline reflect the connection between this passage and the point of the whole letter.

For the group

If you feel comfortable enough with each other, you might begin your meeting by each sharing one example of how your past lives exemplified Titus 3:3, or how God saved you (verse 5) from that state. Then have someone summarize 3:1-11, and move through your meeting as usual. You might want to ask several members to define the word *submission*, and someone else to explain what light the historical background below sheds on Paul's instructions.

Submission

In the Roman Empire, people did not elect imperial judges, representatives to city councils, or any civil officials. Sometimes a law or a legal decision could be changed by a peaceful petition to a governor, but ordinary people were not encouraged to petition. In criminal court, the magistrate generally had unlimited authority,[2] except when a statute gave specific instructions.

With almost no legal ways to express political opinions, people often resorted to riots. In particular, groups who felt their livelihoods threatened were quick to revolt (Acts 19:23-41),[3] and Rome expected civil authorities to be ruthless in maintaining order. An unruly area—as

(continued on page 72)

(continued from page 71)

Crete seems to have been—usually had strict magistrates constantly watching to crush malcontents before a riot erupted.

Squabbles between Christians and Jews or Christians and Gentiles punctuate the book of Acts; they probably occurred everywhere. Pagans regarded Judaism as queer, but at least it was the tradition of the Jews' ancestors. Christianity lacked even that merit. Officially Christianity was legal, but pagans called it a "superstition." Christians refused to attend civic ceremonies or private parties where pagan gods would be honored. Therefore, many people thought Christians were atheistic, unpatriotic, and antisocial—"haters of the human race."[4] Rumors spread that there was cannibalism, human sacrifice, and orgies at Christian meetings, because pagans misunderstood the Lord's Supper and the Love Feast.[5]

The Roman government mistrusted private associations—such as religious, trade, and burial clubs—because they were so often seedbeds of sedition. Such associations were quickly suppressed if any members seemed to "threaten public order or offend public morals."[6] Pagans evidently accused Christians in court of such crimes, in hopes of having the religion itself banned. But Paul had always found the Roman magistrates to be just in observing his lawful conduct and in protecting him from enemies (Acts 18:12-17, 22:22-26:32).

Sometimes, however, although judges acquitted Christians of the original charges, the judges still condemned the Christians for refusing to swear in court by the emperor's guardian spirit.[7] In those cases, Christians submitted to the consequences of breaking the law, but still obeyed God's higher law (see Acts 5:29).

1. Guthrie, page 203.
2. Bruce, *New Testament History*, page 423.
3. Bruce, *New Testament History*, pages 328-330, 427-428.
4. Tacitus, *Annals* xv, 44.5, in Bruce, *New Testament History*, page 425.
5. Chadwick, pages 25-26; Bruce, *New Testament History*, pages 426-427.
6. Bruce, *New Testament History*, page 426.
7. Chadwick, pages 26-28.

LESSON EIGHT

TITUS 3:12-15 AND REVIEW

Last Words

Try to read through the entire book of Titus once more as though you were rereading a treasured letter from a friend. It should be very familiar to you by now, so you should be able to read rapidly. Look for threads that run through the book.

Also, review lesson one, and recall how you summarized each passage in lessons two through seven. Look at any outlines you made.

This may sound like a lot of work, but all of this review will help you make connections among things you've learned and commit important truths to memory.

Study Skill—Comparing Versions
Looking at different translations of the same verse often gives you new perspectives on what the verse may mean.

1. Below are three versions of Titus 3:14. After studying each version, write in your own words what you think verse 14 means.

   Our people must learn to devote themselves to doing what is good, in order that they may provide for daily necessities and not live unproductive lives. NIV

   And let our people also learn to engage in good deeds [or, *occupations*] *to meet pressing needs, that they may not be unfruitful.* NASB

And let our people learn to apply themselves to good deeds [or, *enter honorable occupations*], *so as to help in cases of urgent need, and not to be unfruitful.* RSV

Review

2. In question 6 of lesson six, you let other parts of the New Testament shed light on the letter to Titus. Now review all that the letter says about *doing good* (Titus 1:8,16; 2:3,7,14; 3:1,5,8,14). What are the one or two lessons about doing good that seem most important to you currently?

3. Summarize what the letter teaches about *what a Christian leader should be and do.* (Recall key verses like 1:5-9; 2:1,7,15. Consider words and ideas that Paul repeats.)

4. Paul had a great deal to say to Titus about *arguing* (1:6-7,10; 2:9; 3:2,9-11). Review what he said on this topic, and write here anything you especially want to remember about it.

5. What did you learn about *God* from this letter that you think is especially important?

6. Did you make any other discoveries in your study of Titus that you want to be sure to

For Thought and Discussion: Why do you suppose Paul gave so much instruction about arguing?

remember? If so, you might note them here to reinforce your memory.

____

____

____

____

____

____

Study Skill—Returning to the Purpose
Many teachers of Bible study stress the importance of returning to the author's purpose after detailed study of a book. J. I. Packer calls this the "spiral" approach to Bible study. *Our* purpose for studying the book may not be the same as the author's or first reader's, but their goals should shape how we interpret and apply what they say.

7. In question 10 of lesson one, you defined what seemed to be Paul's overall purpose in his letter to Titus. You also noted the main ideas that leaped out at you on your first reading. Having completed your study, would you revise your view of Paul's main aim? If so, write here your new statement of the letter's purpose.

____

____

____

____

____

____

8. Look back at the questions about the book of Titus that you listed at the end of lesson one (page 17). Also, scan through any questions you may have noted at the ends of other lessons.

Has your study of the book answered those questions? If not, do any of them still seem important to you? If you do still have significant questions, consider possible ways of further study on your own, or with someone who could help you.

9. Look back over the entire study at questions in which you expressed a desire to make some specific personal application. Are you satisfied with your follow-through? Pray about any of those areas that you think you should continue to pursue specifically. (Perhaps something new has come to mind that you would like to concentrate on. If so, bring it before God in prayer as well.) Write here anything you decide to do.

____

____

____

____

____

____

____

10. Have you made any discoveries that you feel will help you become more sensitive to God's work in your life, more able to respond in practical obedience? If so, write it down! This is a major insight!

____

____

____

____

____

____

____

____

Optional Application: **Have you noticed any areas (thoughts, attitudes, opinions, behavior) in which you have changed as a result of your study of Titus? If you have, describe what has happened to you and how God has been at work in your life. You might plan to tell someone.**

For the group

You might organize your discussion around three questions: 1) What have you learned from your study of Titus; 2) How have you changed as a result of your study; and 3) Where will you go from here? You may be more able to see each other's growth than your own. Think about why change has or has not occurred. Try to encourage each other without expecting instant results.

Give everyone a chance to ask questions he or she still has about the book. See if you can plan how to answer them.

Then, evaluate how well your group functioned during your study of Titus. (You might take a whole meeting for this.) Some questions you might ask are:

What did you learn about small group study?
How well did the study help you grasp the book of Titus?
What were the most important truths you discovered together about the Lord?
What did you like best about your meetings?
What did you like least? What would you change?
How well did you meet the goals you set at your first meeting?
What are the members' current needs? What will you do next?

Doing Good

Before he became a Christian, Paul followed the strictest interpretation of the Jewish law: to be righteous before God a person had to do only good, no evil. "Doing good" meant doing what the Jewish law said, with the proper motive of wanting to please God (Galatians 3:10, 5:3).[1] After he became a Christian, Paul taught as a central doctrine that we can be declared righteous before God only by putting faith in Christ's sacrifice (Romans 3:21-28, Galatians 3:10-12). Doing good does not affect whether God loves and accepts us as His children. Even after we are justified by faith, we do not earn God's continu-

(continued on page 79)

(continued from page 78)

ing blessing by works (Galatians 3:1-5).

So what is doing good? And why should we do it, if not to earn God's acceptance? The gentile Cretans would have thought first of the teachings of pagan philosophers. Stoics said that each man should be self-sufficient but should uphold justice, order, reason, and truth. Aristotelians taught the "golden mean"—to avoid excessive love, hate, courage, or cowardice, and to give each man what you owe him. The good citizen was the good man; he obeyed the law, took care of his own needs, and righted injustice within reasonable bounds. He did good because it was his duty as a human, a social being. Living in accord with Reason was the only sensible thing to do.[2]

Paul did not utterly reject these basic notions of what it means to do good—neither Jewish obedience nor pagan justice. Instead, he followed Jesus in going beyond these basics to teach dependence on God and other people, sacrificial love, humility, and "walking by the Spirit." To understand more fully what Paul meant by doing good, see Romans 8:1-14, 12:1-13:10; 2 Corinthians 3:7; Galatians 1:10, 5:13-16. See also Jesus' words in Luke 10:25-42, John 15:1-15.

1. Bruce, *Paul: Apostle of the Heart Set Free*, pages 50-51.
2. Bruce, *New Testament History*, pages 42-47. On Stoicism, see *The Meditations* by Marcus Aurelius. On Aristotle, see his *Nichomachean Ethics*.

STUDY AIDS

For further information on the material covered in this study, you might consider the following sources. If your local bookstore does not have them, you can have the bookstore order them from the publisher, or you can find them in most seminary libraries. Many university and public libraries will also carry these books.

Commentaries on Titus

Fee, Gordon. *1 and 2 Timothy, Titus* (Harper Good News Commentary, Harper and Row, 1984).

Brief, non-technical, verse-by-verse commentary for laymen. Mainly exegesis (explanation of the text), rather than exposition (preaching and application). Based on the Good News Bible, and grounded in sound scholarship to show the Greek behind the translation.

Guthrie, Donald. *Pastoral Epistles* (Tyndale New Testament Commentary, Eerdmans, 1957).

The same type of work as Fee's, except that Guthrie's is based on the King James Version.

Hendriksen, William. *Thessalonians-Titus* (Baker, n.d.).

Hendriksen's commentaries are mainly excellent exposition, rather than exegesis, although sound exegesis lies behind his work. Reads like good sermons on the letters.

Kelly, J. N. D. *A Commentary on the the Pastoral Epistles* (Baker, 1963).

More thorough exegesis than Fee or Guthrie, with more information. Very readable and not lengthy, although Kelly includes in parentheses the ancient sources for his explanations of the text and Paul's world.

Baxter, J. Sidlow. *Explore the Book* (Zondervan, 1960).

This was originally a six-volume survey course of the whole Bible, but it became so popular that Zondervan has printed it in one 1800-page volume since 1966. Baxter does not give verse-by-verse commentary, but instead gives clear broad outlines, overviews of each book, and review questions. Each chapter of Baxter's work is a "lesson" that assigns a portion of Scripture to be read and then gives enough exposition, commentary, and practical application to orient the reader. Baxter was a great preacher, and his style is inspiring. The lesson on Titus is just a few pages long.

Historical Sources

Bruce, F. F. *New Testament History* (Doubleday, 1979).

A readable history of Herodian kings, Roman governors, philosophical schools, Jewish sects, Jesus, the early Jerusalem church, Paul, and early gentile Christianity. Well documented with footnotes for the serious student, but the notes do not intrude.

Bruce, F. F. *Paul, Apostle of the Heart Set Free* (Eerdmans, 1977).

Possibly the best book around on Paul's personality and ideas set in their historical context. Excellent both on Paul's teaching and his times. Very readable.

Harrison, E. F. *Introduction to the New Testament* (Eerdmans, 1971).

History from Alexander the Great—who made Greek culture dominant in the biblical world—through philosophies, pagan and Jewish religion, Jesus' ministry and teaching (the weakest section), and the spread of Christianity. Very good maps and photographs of the land, art, and architecture of New Testament times.

Concordances, Dictionaries, and Handbooks

A *concordance* lists words of the Bible alphabetically along with each verse in which the word appears. It lets you do your own word studies. An *exhaustive* concordance lists every word used in a given translation, while an *abridged* or *complete* concordance omits either some words, some occurrences of the word, or both.

The two best exhaustive concordances are *Strong's Exhaustive Concordance* and *Young's Analytical Concordance to the Bible*. Both are based on the King James Version of the Bible. *Strong's* has an index by which you can find out which Greek or Hebrew word is used in a given English verse. *Young's* breaks up each English word it translates. However, neither concordance requires knowledge of the original language.

Among other good, less expensive concordances, *Cruden's Complete Concordance* is keyed to the King James and Revised Versions, and *The NIV*

Complete Concordance is keyed to the New International Version. These include all references to every word included, but they omit "minor" words. They also lack indexes to the original languages.

A *Bible dictionary* or *Bible encyclopedia* alphabetically lists articles about people, places, doctrines, important words, customs, and geography of the Bible.

The New Bible Dictionary, edited by J. D. Douglas, F. F. Bruce, J. I. Packer, N. Hillyer, D. Guthrie, A. R. Millard, and D. J. Wiseman (Tyndale, 1982) is more comprehensive than most dictionaries. Its 1300 pages include quantities of information along with excellent maps, charts, diagrams, and an index for cross-referencing.

Unger's Bible Dictionary by Merrill F. Unger (Moody, 1979) is a bit shorter, but it has very good maps and diagrams and is available in an inexpensive paperback edition.

The Zondervan Pictorial Encyclopedia edited by Merrill C. Tenney (Zondervan, 1975, 1976) is excellent and exhaustive, and is being revised and updated in the 1980's. However, its five 1000-page volumes are a financial investment, so all but very serious students may prefer to use it at a church, public, college, or seminary library.

Unlike a Bible dictionary in the above sense, *Vine's Expository Dictionary of New Testament Words* by W. E. Vine (various publishers) alphabetically lists major words used in the King James Version and defines each New Testament Greek word that KJV translates with that English word. *Vine's* lists verse references where that Greek word appears, so that you can do your own cross-references and word studies without knowing any Greek.

Handbooks come in various types.

Eerdmans' Handbook to the Bible (1973) begins with brief articles on customs, settings, people, places, and themes of the Bible. Then it comments briefly on each book of the Bible, explaining about the author, date, setting, themes, and key passages. It also includes short articles on archaeology and other topics that shed light on the biblical story. Its timelines are especially good.

The Bible Almanac edited by J. I. Packer, Merrill C. Tenney, and William White, Jr. (Thomas Nelson Press, 1980) is a large, hardbound book of articles on life in Israel, other Old Testament nations, and the Roman Empire. It gives a wealth of information about food, war, transportation, animals, plants, government, women, and so on, as well as brief overviews of Old and New Testament history.

Thomas Nelson also publishes a series of inexpensive paperback handbooks edited by Packer, Tenney, and White. *The World of the New Testament* is relevant to Titus.

A good *Bible atlas* can be a great aid to understanding where Paul traveled, where Jesus ministered, and so forth. Among the many good ones are *Baker's Bible Atlas* edited by Charles F. Pfeiffer (1979). It has fairly good maps with explanatory text on most major places in the Bible at various times in history.

For Small Group Leaders

How to Lead Small Group Bible Studies (NavPress, 1982).

Just 71 pages. It hits the highlights of how to get members acquainted, ask questions, plan lessons, deal with interpersonal relations, and handle prayer.

The Small Group Leader's Handbook by Steve Barker et al. (InterVarsity, 1982).

Written by an InterVarsity small group with college students primarily in mind. It includes more than the above book on small group dynamics and how to lead in light of them, and many ideas for worship, building community, and outreach. It has a good chapter on doing inductive Bible study.

Getting Together: A Guide for Good Groups by Em Griffin (InterVarsity, 1982).

Applies to all kinds of groups, not just Bible studies. From his own experience, Griffin draws deep insights into why people join groups; how people relate to each other; and principles of leadership, decision-making, and discussions. It is fun to read, not highbrow, but its 229 pages will take more time than the above books.

The Small Group Letter (NavPress).

Unique. Its six pages per issue, ten issues per year are packed with practical ideas for asking questions, planning Bible studies, leading discussions, dealing with group dynamics, encouraging spiritual growth, doing outreach, and so on. It stays up to date because writers always discuss what they are currently doing as small group members and leaders. To subscribe, write to *The Small Group Letter*, Subscription Services, Post Office Box 1164, Dover, New Jersey 07801.

Bible Study Methods

Braga, James. *How to Study the Bible* (Multnomah, 1982).

Clear chapters on a variety of approaches to Bible study: synthetic, geographical, cultural, historical, doctrinal, practical, and so on. Designed to help the ordinary person without seminary training to use these approaches.

Fee, Gordon, and Douglas Stuart. *How to Read the Bible For All Its Worth* (Zondervan, 1982).

After explaining in general what interpretation (exegesis) and application (hermeneutics) are, Fee and Stuart offer chapters on interpreting and applying the different kinds of writing in the Bible: Epistles, Gospels, Old Testament Law, Old Testament narrative, the Prophets, Psalms, Wisdom, and Revelation. Fee and Stuart also suggest good commentaries on each biblical book. They write as conservative scholars who personally recognize Scripture as God's Word for their daily lives.

Jensen, Irving L. *Independent Bible Study* (Moody, 1963), and *Enjoy Your Bible* (Moody, 1962).

The former is a comprehensive introduction to the inductive Bible study method, expecially the use of synthetic charts. The latter is a simpler introduction to the subject.

Wald, Oletta. *The Joy of Discovery in Bible Study* (Augsburg, 1975).

Wald focuses on issues such as how to observe all that is in a text, how to ask questions of a text, how to use grammar and passage structure to see the writer's point, and so on. Very helpful on these subjects.